What Space Between Us

David Rushmer

*What Space
Between Us*

Shearsman Books

First published in the United Kingdom in 2022 by
Shearsman Books
PO Box 4239
Swindon
SN3 9FN

Shearsman Books Ltd Registered Office
30–31 St. James Place, Mangotsfield, Bristol BS16 9JB
(this address not for correspondence)

www.shearsman.com

ISBN 978-1-84861-829-9

Copyright © David Rushmer, 2022

The right of David Rushmer to be identified as the author of this work has been asserted by him in accordance with the Copyrights, Designs and Patents Act of 1988.
All rights reserved.

ACKNOWLEDGEMENTS
Some of these poems were previously published in the following journals: *BlazeVOX, Epizootics, E.ratio, Human Repair Kit, Molly Bloom, Otata, Otoliths,* and *Shearsman*.

A poetry sequence (with added photographs by the author) was created using the italicized words from sections 1 & 2 of this book and published as a limited edition pamphlet, *The Empty Centre* by Aphonic Space, USA, 2021.

Cover photograph by David Rushmer

Contents

What Space Between Us

A Matter of Memory / 9
What Space Between Us / 10
The Way / 11
Intercourse / 12
Forming Principles / 14
Where We Vanish To / 16
What Matters / 19
Rising in the Sap (after Sappho) / 20
The Gesture / 26
Dictate / 28
The Death Sensations / 29
Particles and Atoms / 30
When Night Fell / 32
A Matter of Silence / 33
Placed (for Wang Bang) / 34
Kindling / 35
Erased Matter / 38
A Remembering of Soft Hair / 40
A Book of Skin, or Liberation Through Seeing/
Hearing During the Intermediate State / 42
Panes (after James Joyce) / 45

Depth Charge

Depth Charge / 49
Wounds / 53
Fathom / 55

Tongue to Tongue / 57
Night Flowered / 58
Behind the Eyes / 59

Returning Breath

Returning Breath / 63
The Filament's Heat / 69
Darkening / 78
Lightforce / 79
Still Time / 90
White Drift / 96
Meeting Me Halfway / 102

WHAT SPACE BETWEEN US

A Matter of Memory

      to *imagine*
            a matter of memory:

    our bodies
    the archives
        a book of flesh

            its secret gardens
                  plowing speech

    to penetrate the literal absent
& lend *your body* to the sky

What Space Between Us

language

    a stone

    total

weightlessness

    attachment

    the circle
        one becomes

violence

    I was the *object*

the anguish of *disappearing*

pain of our speech

The Way

from the *unfurling*

        ignition of wings

the wind
        takes our *breath* away

waiting   for *the sky*

        to remove its mask

        exhale into stone

time buried in its folds

muscle *of* earth

        showing its *scars*

the body's imprint

Intercourse

speak, then,
    of the disappeared
        of disappearance.

            a beginning
            swells

    this is your
            vast abyss
        of loss
        stripped of certainty

      in empty halls
           of language

      a moment of calm in white flowers

words dilute on the breeze
detached from their brute
        energy
        creating
a world without us.

      what makes you forget
           this memory

      the vanishing point
      the tongue
  a singular event

                    opening
                the wind

    forgotten
    drafts
    of light
    becoming
                            intercourse

Forming Principles

    forming
    principles of
        sublimation

        burst to give light
   moments us
                          oozing
                      discourse

          crepuscular
               guttering
to drain the blood

                      air

        into flame
       a vanishing sequence
     instead of being
      a skin
  over surface
     withdraws his fingers
        to the touch
     into film
     a vision
     in which vision
reflects

                        the disappearance
                    of the real world

viscous universe
                consuming
            substances
                of beauty
                that gathered
            fragrances
            to inhale the skull

Where We Vanish to

I

There is no
        longing
    for a form

        another way of seeing
        the shadow
        approaching
slow cancellation
    eroded moment
    skins the expression
        endemic

        hungering space
        will open up
    electrical forces
    featureless remnants
between two mirrors
a whole series of absences
        spectral

the *touch* of light
    & ghosts remain
    undermining the present being
    collapsed
by *the disappearance.*

II

There is no
 longer
    a state

    exhausted
    insomniac
    eroticized

    a figure of speech
    vanished

    writing
scraping my face
        away

What Matters

    centred on bone
    the other
                as
lightness

                becomes
                a motion
    to say,

                a substance
    to be observed
                remaining visible
                in the form
    to butcher
imaginary matter

    doubt
        and language.

/vanish

    beyond themselves

        light

          must come
                  beyond the shape

                        and open
            the eye
        as pattern
            activity

    that might be what matters

                          dissolved in the
        voicing.

Rising in the Sap (after Sappho)

I

who is gone
toward

        your gracious form
        on the
        tongue

waiting
   blasts of wind

that
sing us.

II

    carried you
        to garlands of
delicate longing.

    we were absent.

no sound.

      moon
  and her light
barefoot
on the black earth

    broken chambers
      of stars
        poured upon
   the song

   dripping gold   weaving sleep.

III

      blowing
in this place

   to shine
   further sorrow

      breathed the sun
            to her ankles

         to become
         dawn again

   the brilliance new

the heart
they become.

IV

dream of
    blazing

blossom
    delight
      in your soft hands
                flower
          shaped
       to listen.

V

    she spoke
of nowhere
with slender limbs

           wind falling
                  burned with longing
                  to touch the sky
                            like roses
            wrapped in
                  the memory of you.

VI

float
deep sound necklaces
        of wings
   under skin

   eyes
   greener than grass

   moonform
   on the earth

   dripping winds
      burn me
          pour my thoughts

                           wings
for a day.

The Gesture

the gesture
                                           producing
                                displacement

     lip service
                              engendering
                                              objects
circulating a certain
              resignation
sings
      the unseen,

              meatspace
              of a
                    brutal friend.

II

    out of nowhere
            sonic lace

        becoming a part of
        the *shores*
            of accidental
                winter

      carrying

                within its core
                within his belly

the bullet's *teeth*

Dictate

I

    empty body to the *skin*

            begin to flow

  to collect the loss
            against the mark.

        Others.

        sang of its body.

II

    I heard the rain

          spoken

        in *memory*
        only

  from breath
      the only organ

The Death Sensations

The *death*
sensations.

fingers in the room
    that touch
        with some
            dark
  practice
beyond
      an infinity
if you stand between two mirrors

a skin guttering
      the culmination
      forming
      principles of coagula

  whose *body* all things
have seen
      reflected
    in another distance
    complete

Particles and Atoms

light of morning

        swells

makes possible a *hovering*
of the form

a continuum
    between
        patterns

magnified *in the absence*

    thirsting

found
    matter

II

        to put a skin over the place
        that resembled a movement

        a place *where you too*
reside

    another force
        in the branch

blossoming

    breath
        of snow

When Night Fell

        voice
                haunted
                former beauty
        in these veins

     When night fell
I remained

        singing your name in the silence of it

            rapture
of this disappearance

when *she unfolded*
        living memory
            collided

     "what could your hands teach us if you had not vanished?"

A Matter of Silence

                      speaking of

                              lilacs

                                  a bruise of magic
                  on the *tongue*

            mirror

       with wings *cut*

Placed (for Wang Bang)

    a beautiful place (with you

           sun leaked
                floating

    we saw *light*   winged,
                         morning
forever haunted

ghosts into bone

    love   of all
        spirit

        the pink sky   fluttering

memory of my blood
                blushed

Kindling

        transparency of
the form

    that carries a body
I cannot separate from

   liquid night
   of graveyards

    hovering

   this sky

        & the music I chose
        from the inside and out

interpreted and
   translated
   bliss

        your hand
        sounding
            the sunlight we are making

   "rubbing till your work is gone"

II

    to disappear

           into
           forms

                between
                speech
                roots

                and
       silences
            to come
                  spark across bridges
                      collapsing

       to catch one's breath
                in a mirror
                    of rain

conceiving
    the mind
    in each
    droplet

    into likeness
        of likeness

collision, *of fragments*

"to burn up, in a gesture
outside the body"

Erased Matter

we have taken to the air.
no matter.
object, or body

    a book of skin
             where it flows

                    "to slowly wend its way
an umbilical between *worlds*…

              …with both ends burning"

      the vessels are nothing
           whiteness is an ideal
                rather be the flame
                wanting the skin
                        to become
                        this subtle fluid
                        in memory only

            the *ignition*,
                      in the blood

    the spoke
becomes
another form in aural space

                          "we are already dissolved
        in the voice.

                                      an annihilation of space
              enlightened
                    of elements
            the unseen
                  focus
             opening
        this hole
in which I am *floating*

       the message
of the body
                  seen
    as interior space

           the sky
            you spoke

                            to remain fluid
               in a kind of music

           a matter of memory:
           to penetrate the literal absent
   nothing remains
     around the meat
               with their perfume
                 between my lips
               this hole, this torn
                         black sky   open
     from somewhere else
       folded

       breathing flows

A Remembering of Soft Hair

"He wrote me
        in
   a kind of white light

      remembering thirst
      wind driven

    to fill a *silence*
with strangers

when stars explode
      into
    neighbouring material

we connect to *distant* objects by mouth

    perfect diction

    the theory
    physical barrier

       of the *skin*
          of the sky

possibility and impossibility

   the flesh of it

      particles of light
         on the periphery

         memory of soft hair

"soft hair" is a term coined by Stephen Hawking to describe some of the particle's information that may be left around the event horizon of a black hole.

A Book of Skin, or Liberation Through Seeing/Hearing During the Intermediate State

a book of skin.

    There is another

    where it flows.

    to imagine
           a book

   your body

          death
             beyond

              touching
              the disappearance.

                a vanishing

                to say,
                to be observed

                or to butcher
       the eye

II

                sonic
        shores
        of light

    carrying
teeth

slowly
pushing through you

      skins
      dreaming

                    hovering

          bardo form

                collapsing
                        mirrors
            in the hand

III

      When night fell

               she *unfolded*

Panes (after James Joyce)

                night   :
          returning   meat

to enter into
        the illusion
                of sympathies

        she comes
        between our phrases,

skulled
        voices:

        sharpening their eyes
in slow circles,

        clouds meet before time
        to speak

of
            lace]
        your performance
            of smoke

```
            moving in
                        some trembling language

        about the body

    movement of the limbs, passing
            whirling,
                        falling again to earth


    A moment
withdrawn,
            —  in a moment. I remember
            I remember
                the body
        as a light shower
                returning
                        promises of Spring,
                    night silence
            under waves
                    the eyes
                    entering
            stone.




                                windows
                    to an air of perfumes
```

DEPTH CHARGE

Depth Charge

I

from where
    I stand
    nothing remains
        in the mirror
        to speak to me

    collapsed inside
        just wind and bone
        opening *towards*
            bloody morning
    in dreams
    more beautiful
around the meat.

II

blood shared
    I hold her
        ghost
        escaping
        with perfume
            in bloom

        the rivers, and the bodies
          beneath
          hair pulled back
            in the sun

skinned tongue
in solitude
I enter
    and make him speak
        between my lips
  mouthing
the game.

III

       A flowered hand
            ripped   *from the pink*
               ballet
          of fists
       this hole, this torn
       air
where I return
          my meat
             further
          beneath whispers.

IV

borders, change
    eat the night
        passing through
    half asleep, a bird
        toward the open window

        the corridor
         of wind
         driving
         black sky   *open.*

Wounds

wounds

        create an origin
the writer
orientated
                  the fragile
before the eruption
partakes
    in a betrayal
        to remain fluid
            keeping open the possibility
            the event
of *the impossible*
        discharged through writing

        a window
        the locus within
        exploring
      the moment
        founded
    escapes where the act
      sexual   abjection
        pushed to its extreme

      forbidden darkness
    elements
      of arrested code
     grounds
          against his boot

       a place for myself
            seeks to bleed
externalization   beyond the trauma
          the unfolding
    resembles
    that sexual pleasure
         close to nothing

    eventually entering
      a moment
    cause of the *broken*
rapist   in my future
les yeux de dieu

    I see
        bright
            gilded
                hunger

a body claimed
in a kind of music
      to control rhythm
to heal the sound

Fathom

-

    draw and slip
       my own
dark chambers

-

    walls dismembered
body spread, gaping

    I watch the page of writing
       unfurl in myself

-

      blue eyes
         with another sleep
       gusts of the sea breeze

his entire body
   a theatre
      of full light

-

    disappear in such *violence*
       disappear to another

- *burning* all
    who persuade
    before I write it
into laughter

- what sound, the deep
  discovers
      from behind the act
          located

  breathing flows
      in folded waves

Tongue to Tongue

language to *language,* body to body
      the cosmic distance

           so frail beneath my fingers
           created dust

the page of writing
      in myself

      skinned

Night Flowered

        night flowered
        in the hand
         itching. In the voice
     and this caress
     one speaks sheets
        of the dream
   from somewhere else

breath-wall

absorbs the cry

     unfolding stars
        flowing

         skins
              onward,

      my dead birds
          fluted
          through
     dreaming
  blue eyes
     folded.

Behind the Eyes

I only glimpsed
      that fragile
      fluttering of eyelashes

and speak or paint or dream
beyond *atrocities*
      before him

         "every girl is the queen of the world"

a ladder
      of wild grasses
      enters *an unknown*
            sleep
      to prepare our arrival

my bare hands
tighten
his breaking voice
      you're feeling
      against the wall

                half of
      my body   –   I scrape my knees

wait for the darkness
the small veins
        spread
    in the sky
    cover my body
          everything that is naked

     my head
         entirely vision
             hunting
                  a space
somewhere *inside the mouth*

RETURNING BREATH

"...*poems are* en route; *they are headed towards...with manmade stars flying overhead, unsheltered even by the traditional tent of the sky, exposed in an unsuspected, terrifying way, carry their existence into language, racked by reality and in search of it."*
　　　　　　Paul Celan – from *Collected Prose*
　　　　　　　translated by Rosemarie Waldrop

Returning Breath

•

        hunger
the word

    wandering mirror
       of your hand

   drifting

       hailstone
       in the air

    without language

•

   the morning
     songs

    your speech
deep crystal

II

•
    blown empty

                    the mouth
                    the sky

         silk and
blood

language
  you burn

•
    eyelash memory
      I held you

    our mouths
          skin   sound

        light
    sinks
with us.

III

-
    empty the shadow
        from smoke
        they eat

-
        you
                also   in
            language skull

heaven's fists
    white

    endless ghosts
soundlessly
    bloom
    in the breath

    your speech
invented
scars

IV

•

        writing burns
it's memory

        full lung
        in the opened book

something
        black
              drinks
bullet holes
& you forget where memory catches
it's breath

•

    punctuation
    your wounds talking

    your hands
        orbiting
        invisible
      circle language

V

•

       glowing
in the
marrow

     blood

           wings the breath

  shot from the world
      & the silence
you empty into

•

    threaded kisses
       with heavens' mirror

the earth pushed out
     in your wounds

VI

•

    once
     I

        was

light

The Filament's Heat

•

       brightness
floodlights
           the sentence

                  raining knives.

•

    this world
        burrows colours
        the comet cipher

   light
of our houses.

•

your reflection
    in the mouth
    blows visible
        the marrow

    stuttering
        smoke spasms
    deep painted,
    eternalized

   sing the bone
      dripping
         in the arm.

•

     deep inside
 driving
you wake
 deeper
 in the branch
    escaping

•

   whisper of leaves
embrace

skinned mirror

II

-
        empty mouths

hatched
      the blue gull
           eternities

-
      between   pauses

     the constellation,
light rained spore,

white passages
     to a secret world.

-
     tongue of night
     the dark orbit
     around
          the second skull

- sky

        into

                    heart

-

          the sound wall
     colliding   naked
     behind
     the breathing

-

        at

the
place

they all come

           injected
     her lace

-

     darkness
     mothered

     folds
     the path

      bite
              blood
                        bouquets

the vocal space,
the eternities
budding

III

•

        winds' lung
                collapses

shells
another figure
      accompanied
           through the void

•

        breathed death
           from me,

           into you,

  streams
      by the flood
      blooms
      on each sepal
in each white stone
a wish
      skirts
      your eye

horizons emptied

IV

•

unsheathed eye
      thrust
            behind
            his mantle

•

  night
     in the fingertip

  teases the dew

  the moon
pelted
     together
     from
     twilight
swallowing its teeth

•

on the mirror,
    bolt of lightning,
bones harvested
    before the remainder
        is blown
      under blood

∙

      beyond
    the chambers
the memory of matter

time unsheathed
      in the sky tissue

V

•

speech burning

    the lightning of bodies
    ignited deep lattice
        in
        the breath

    your tongue
    you hold
    darkening

        bird song
        by
        your
        own hand buried

Darkening

-
    hanging
                toward us

the day
        bleeding
            light

    the sky
            written upon
                stone

-
    you too were
        memory

        a breath
in your language

Lightforce

-
    day&night
            birthmarked

            drove
            the rivers
                    melting
    whose necklaces
    disconnected
            asunder

-
            blown
    into
    deep orbit

            the birth moment
                    stone from the
                            sound

-
            heaven

    the death
            I
            carry

a finger's tip
        in lost matter

II

•

death was
a conversation
    behind the curtain

pearl

        among these stones

        white wound
           where
             I forget myself

•

something
    rushes through
    the wings

    spreads
    the draft
in the heart

        sings
the burn

fireblooms

   threadbare angel
      by lightning
          formed.

III

•

out of yourself

    light
    swimming

        drifting
        soundless

        stars
  pour
  an echo
of your face
where I threw myself toward
    what I become

    by the world
        blood promised

IV

●

    the eternities
        and beyond
              blaze
              buried
              spectral
              light
              of
    margins

a voice
    driving
        into your hand

●

              blue eye
    distance
    where you open up
        in blood

        the blast
            of
respiration
in the chambers
throws
the swarm

						together

				sound shadows
	webbing between
					light

V

•
                each breath
of the chamber,

the heart
the frost

       flowers the script

•

angel in orbit
two
planet
    eyes

       blind

stone pierced blood
           harvests
       stillness
       in the fire sung

   •

       voiced
       from the deep

        single truth
        of a
                shell
        night
bellows
loss

unveiled
        in its breath

•

earth's
    lung
        on the
        wing

snow
from its own eye

to light
        the tear

•

thunder
    spoken
    before mirrors

                frozen blue
    in the mouth
        pollen in the skull

        language
       into
              dust

              blown
into the flowering

VI

•

               eyes
      rest the gaze

    silence
          snowed

        dream
        the
        bones

         clawing
the sky

Still Time

•
        catch yourself
        in
        speech
shattered
        moons
  and
        nothingness

blue,   blue
                flame
you roll
      inward
      in a dream
windblown

•
the choir
      of rain
              shall emerge
      out of the gills
      copulating
      beyond you

•
white
  ocean

  come
by eternity
  & the marrow

  when I touch
you

•

mouth
  of
  time mute stars

    plundered
  of sleep forms
joined up in me

•

we are
the thorn of
      time
  inserted into
    speech

    blood
glimpsed
  in lightning

-
                    your eye
            in the circle

                open

layered
        with fire

-
                behind death
                thunder
                        hollows

II

  •

       the
            tomb
            opens
                    toward me
      swells
      our mouths
in whiteness

  •

the swarm
      where
      I forget from
      where
the radiance
orphaned
      into the seeing
           pores

  •

     bright
abyss
      in glowing
      empty
         time

   I lose you
   in snow

   whiteness
      open, forever

the constellation

    the wound

      marks
      tuning

      draws the
      circle

    silencing

•

   star
you carry
infinite
   pulse

skin
   swimming
   into

a
fist

III

•

outside
        the singing
    hands
        half rupture
        the
earth

•

you hear
            the world
    in its
dwarfing whisper
   in the
      chamber

          soon it will be
dancing
toward
the invisible
        wind

     behind the eye

White Drift

•

    air

aflame in the wind

        open mouthed

•

blood sews the voice
        with white needle

•

        your shadow
            recognizes you
    in the passage through
veins blossomed

•

my mouth skins

    buried light

II

•

    darkness thorned

           between the face
&
your scream
below
      the fingers

•

      the sky
           hangs

under your breath

•

blackbirds
    drifting night

mouthed
        the sorrow blown
        substance

III

•

sink myself into
                    snow

wave of black bullet

       astral memory

            arrowing
      the bone

      and
      our silk feelings of
          sleep

•

      abyss
            fluttered

echoing

IV

•

                        bloom
              by tongue

              leaf
              and mirror

        messengers
by matter   filtered

              air
              shaped
                      hand

                      deep in
                      yourself

     blown empty

V

•

        mirror

a skin you
        push through

articulations,

                ghost
      my
      insides

                blood
      rotating

Meeting Me Halfway

"offspring, glowing
appears *eternal*."

I

      (language, a physical shape within breath…)

         going to their death together
the grave
    this *passage* opens
       to stone
    beyond

I have placed
    you
    among others

    perhaps
       in order
       to breathe

in other words.

•

    return *to*
       time forgotten

II

(language as shape, a direction of breath…)

        I am looking for
the place,
        his grave
                we locate

        his step
                the sky below

sudden *opening*
        of an encounter

                a turning of our breath
                      in the same direction.

•

        our origin
      speaks only
            of the limits
of the possibilities it opens
        in the encounter

        another figure
                achieved by the eye

                        questioning
only *the space* of speaking.

•

      you come
into
question

open, empty
    in the light

    time
    a circle
of

       the impossible
touched.

www.ingramcontent.com/pod-product-compliance
Lightning Source LLC
Chambersburg PA
CBHW031636160426
43196CB00006B/444